Student Workbook

PACEMAKER®

Basic English Grammar

PEARSON
AGS Globe

Shoreview, MN

1-800-992-0244
www.agsglobe.com

Table of Contents

Chapter 1   Nouns

Workbook Activity 1   Finding the Nouns
Workbook Activity 2   Finding Common and Proper Nouns
Workbook Activity 3   Identifying Concrete and Abstract Nouns
Workbook Activity 4   Using Singular and Plural Nouns
Workbook Activity 5   Creating Plural Nouns
Workbook Activity 6   Possessive or Plural Nouns?

Chapter 2   Pronouns

Workbook Activity 7   Using Pronouns
Workbook Activity 8   Using Personal Pronouns
Workbook Activity 9   Finding Relative Pronouns
Workbook Activity 10   Using Pronouns That Ask Questions
Workbook Activity 11   Identifying Demonstrative Pronouns
Workbook Activity 12   Using Indefinite Pronouns
Workbook Activity 13   Recognizing Pronouns in Contractions

Chapter 3   Adjectives

Workbook Activity 14   Identifying Adjectives
Workbook Activity 15   Identifying and Using Articles
Workbook Activity 16   Using Proper and Common Nouns as Adjectives
Workbook Activity 17   Using Possessive Nouns and Pronouns as Adjectives
Workbook Activity 18   Using Numbers and Indefinite Pronouns as Adjectives
Workbook Activity 19   Using Demonstrative Adjectives
Workbook Activity 20   Using Adjectives to Make Comparisons

Chapter 4   Action Verbs

Workbook Activity 21   Using Action Verbs
Workbook Activity 22   Using Simple and Perfect Tenses
Workbook Activity 23   Identifying Irregular Verbs
Workbook Activity 24   Using Progressive Forms
Workbook Activity 25   Making Subjects and Verbs Agree
Workbook Activity 26   Using the Verb *Do*
Workbook Activity 27   Using Conditional Verbs
Workbook Activity 28   Identifying Active and Passive Verbs

Table of Contents, continued

Chapter 5   State-of-Being Verbs

Workbook Activity 29   Identifying State-of-Being Verbs
Workbook Activity 30   Exploring State-of-Being Verb Tense
Workbook Activity 31   Identifying Verbs as Action or State of Being

Chapter 6   Adverbs

Workbook Activity 32   Identifying Adverbs
Workbook Activity 33   Finding Adverbs of Degree
Workbook Activity 34   Identifying Adverbs of Negation
Workbook Activity 35   Using Adverbs to Compare
Workbook Activity 36   Recognizing Adverbs

Chapter 7   Prepositional Phrases

Workbook Activity 37   Identifying Prepositions
Workbook Activity 38   Recognizing the Object of the Preposition
Workbook Activity 39   Recognizing Adjective Phrases
Workbook Activity 40   Adding Adverb Phrases
Workbook Activity 41   Using Prepositional Phrases Correctly
Workbook Activity 42   Identifying Prepositions and Adverbs

Chapter 8   Conjunctions and Interjections

Workbook Activity 43   Using Coordinating Conjunctions
Workbook Activity 44   Using Correlative Conjunctions
Workbook Activity 45   Recognizing Subordinating Conjunctions
Workbook Activity 46   Using Interjections

Chapter 9   Sentences

Workbook Activity 47   Recognizing Sentences
Workbook Activity 48   Finding Subjects in Sentences
Workbook Activity 49   Adding the Predicate of a Sentence
Workbook Activity 50   Identifying the Purposes of Sentences
Workbook Activity 51   Identifying Simple and Compound Sentences

Table of Contents, continued

Chapter 10   Sentence Patterns

Workbook Activity 52	Using Intransitive Verbs
Workbook Activity 53	Diagramming Sentences with Intransitive Verbs
Workbook Activity 54	Using Direct Objects
Workbook Activity 55	Diagramming Sentences with Direct Objects
Workbook Activity 56	Using Indirect Objects
Workbook Activity 57	Diagramming Sentences with Indirect Objects
Workbook Activity 58	Using Object Complements
Workbook Activity 59	Diagramming Sentences with Object Complements
Workbook Activity 60	Using Predicate Nouns
Workbook Activity 61	Diagramming Sentences with Predicate Nouns
Workbook Activity 62	Using Predicate Adjectives
Workbook Activity 63	Diagramming Sentences with Predicate Adjectives

Chapter 11   Complex Sentences

Workbook Activity 64	Using Phrases and Clauses
Workbook Activity 65	Identifying Adverb Clauses
Workbook Activity 66	Using Noun Clauses
Workbook Activity 67	Identifying Appositives and Nouns of Direct Address
Workbook Activity 68	Identifying Adjective Clauses
Workbook Activity 69	Identifying Complex Sentences
Workbook Activity 70	Identifying Compound-Complex Sentences

Chapter 12   Verbal Phrases

Workbook Activity 71	Identifying Infinitives and Infinitive Phrases
Workbook Activity 72	Recognizing Gerunds and Gerund Phrases
Workbook Activity 73	Identifying Participles and Participle Phrases

Finding the Nouns

Directions Underline all of the nouns in each sentence.

1. Yoshi and her mother went to the mall.

2. Many tourists have visited Niagara Falls.

3. Richard found the note taped to his door.

4. Mrs. Parham thanked George for his politeness.

5. Cindy and her family are moving to Kansas.

6. Jose found his wallet under the couch.

7. The audience cheered the violinist.

8. Lucy thought the price of the shirt was too high.

9. Walter has a good knowledge of football.

10. Walden Pond shone in the sunlight.

11. John Adams was our second president.

12. Lisa had a dream about her Spanish test.

13. Andre found a ring with a red stone.

14. Hard work will help Chad win the race.

15. Julio invited his friends to the party.

16. Serena took the atlas off the shelf.

17. Red Knight is my favorite singing group.

18. The soldier received a medal for bravery.

19. The big horse easily jumped the fence.

20. The crowd watched the game with excitement.

Finding Common and Proper Nouns

Directions On each line, write a proper noun for each common noun.

1. grocery store _______________________________________

2. actress _______________________________________

3. TV show _______________________________________

4. city _______________________________________

5. river _______________________________________

6. automobile _______________________________________

7. doctor _______________________________________

8. language _______________________________________

9. holiday _______________________________________

10. song _______________________________________

Directions On each line, write a common noun for each proper noun.

11. Los Angeles _______________________________________

12. Garth Brooks _______________________________________

13. *Oliver Twist* _______________________________________

14. National Museum of Natural History _______________________

15. James Avenue _______________________________________

16. Montana _______________________________________

17. Friday _______________________________________

18. Thanksgiving _______________________________________

19. March _______________________________________

20. White House _______________________________________

Identifying Concrete and Abstract Nouns

Directions On each line, write an abstract noun that belongs in each group. Study the examples in parentheses.

1. action (pace, process) _______________________

2. quality (heroism, confidence) _______________________

3. quantity (ounce, weight) _______________________

4. time (hour, Thursday) _______________________

5. feeling (joy, sorrow) _______________________

Directions On each line, write a concrete noun that belongs in each group. Look at the examples in parentheses.

6. drink (lemonade, milk) _______________________

7. tree (oak, pine) _______________________

8. animal (moose, panda) _______________________

9. tool (hammer, ax) _______________________

10. building (school, stadium) _______________________

Directions Underline the abstract noun in each pair.

11. doctor, health

12. humor, smile

13. flag, freedom

14. pain, bruise

15. family, love

Using Singular and Plural Nouns

Directions Change each noun in parentheses to its plural form. Write the plural form on the line.

1. He wanted three (wish). _______________________

2. There were four (penny) on the floor. _______________________

3. The (monkey) swung through the trees. _______________________

4. The (house) were built of brick. _______________________

5. The team had three (loss) this week. _______________________

6. The students took two (quiz) each week. _______________________

7. Trevor lost his house (key). _______________________

8. These (knife) are not sharp enough. _______________________

9. The recipe required two (tomato). _______________________

10. All the (shoe) in the store were on sale. _______________________

11. Sixteen (baby) were born yesterday. _______________________

12. My parents pay state and local (tax). _______________________

13. The wind blew the (leaf) off the trees. _______________________

14. They painted the (bench) in the park. _______________________

15. Do you think cats have nine (life)? _______________________

Creating Plural Nouns

Directions Change each noun in parentheses to its plural form. Write the plural form on the line.

1. Wool comes from (sheep). _______________________

2. The (goose) flew south for the winter. _______________________

3. The (child) played games at the park. _______________________

4. The (mouse) surrounded the trash cans. _______________________

5. The ground felt hot on his (foot). _______________________

Directions Underline the plural form of each proper noun.

6. September: Septembers, Septemberes

7. Friday: Fridayes, Fridays

8. the Marsh family: the Marshes, the Marshs

9. the Pierson family: the Piersons, the Piersones

10. fox: foxs, foxes

Directions Find the mistake in each sentence. Then, write the sentence correctly.

11. My favorite movies are from the 1980's.

____

12. Raul was proud to get two B's on his report card.

____

13. Students were allowed to retake the quiz if they scored in the 60's.

____

14. I want to buy my first house when I am in my 30's.

____

15. Cheryl was in the 20cs when she lost count of the toothpicks.

____

Possessive or Plural Nouns?

Directions Underline the correct form of the words in parentheses.

1. Paul said that one (band's, bands) music was best.

2. The (childrens', children's) books are at school.

3. Lily found a (mouse's, mouses) nest in the grass.

4. The (hikers, hiker's) reached the top of the mountain.

5. Have you seen the (men's, mens') baseball uniforms?

6. This (snakes, snake's) skin is striped.

7. Have you seen (Jean's, Jeans') scarf?

8. The (coach's, coaches) whistle is loud.

9. Lightning struck the (trees, tree's) trunk.

10. One (team's, teams') score was the best.

11. A small dinosaur ate the (plant's, plants) stem.

12. John put the collar around the (cats, cat's) neck.

13. These (books, books') are expensive.

14. My (friends, friend's) house is very comfortable.

15. That (fires', fire's) heat warms the room.

Using Pronouns

Directions Underline the pronouns in each sentence. Then draw an arrow from each pronoun to its antecedent. There may be more than one pronoun in a sentence.

EXAMPLE Alice saw her mother.

1. Joe said to Bob, "I hope you have fun."

2. Mrs. Brandt said she would not give homework on weekends.

3. It was the best game Carlos had seen.

4. The boys shouted when they were ready.

5. When Lucy found the pin, she put it on the table.

6. Did Lee open his present?

7. Mr.Wardrop picked up his hat.

8. Meg and Sally said, "We had a great time!"

9. The students ate their lunch in the cafeteria.

10. Ellen thought she would leave now for work.

11. When the vase fell, it broke into pieces.

12. Tom asked Pam if she liked the story.

13. Pedro took his dog to the vet.

14. The day was windy, but it was warm.

15. Marat unpacked his suitcase and put it in the closet.

16. Tony said he would mail the letter.

17. Tina said she was hungry.

18. Terry and Paul found their books.

19. Sue said, "Please call me tomorrow."

20. Mrs. Parsons told Jan, "I am coming."

Using Personal Pronouns

Directions Read each pair of sentences. Underline the sentence in each pair that uses the correct pronoun.

EXAMPLE Adam took a picture of him family.
<u>Adam took a picture of his family.</u>

1. Ben likes animals and he wants to be a vet.
Ben likes animals and him wants to be a vet.

2. I found a notebook and asked Corine, "Is this your's?"
I found a notebook and asked Corine, "Is this yours?"

3. Kevin painted the room hisself.
Kevin painted the room himself.

4. Jamal asked us to go to the concert.
Jamal asked we to go to the concert.

5. Armando is very proud of his cooking skills.
Armando is very proud of him cooking skills.

6. When the Harrisons moved to Phoenix, they bought a house.
When the Harrisons moved to Phoenix, them bought a house.

7. Coach Kim said to Leslie, "Your can win this race!"
Coach Kim said to Leslie, "You can win this race!"

8. They cooked dinner themself.
They cooked dinner themselves.

9. Alex worked hard on he project.
Alex worked hard on his project.

10. Jack and me will be there at noon.
Jack and I will be there at noon

Directions Write the compound personal pronoun that completes each sentence. Write *myself, ourselves, yourself, himself, herself, itself,* or *themselves* on the line.

11. I accidentally cut _______________________ while slicing potatoes.

12. Let the dog entertain _______________________ because we are busy right now.

13. You should make a note to remind _______________________ to take out the trash.

14. We treated _______________________ to milkshakes after a hard day of work.

15. Abe moved the large couch by _______________________ .

Finding Relative Pronouns

Directions Underline the relative pronoun in each sentence. Draw an arrow from the pronoun to its antecedent.

EXAMPLE I like the picture <u>that</u> is hanging in the den.

1. My sister, who is seventeen, just got her driver's license.

2. My glasses, which I need for reading, are broken.

3. The party that we planned to attend was called off.

4. The family that lives next door has three dogs and two cats.

5. The girl who sits in the first seat is late.

6. The shoes that Charlotte wore looked very comfortable.

7. The front porch, which is shaded by trees, is a nice place to relax.

8. The flowers that are on the front porch need water.

9. People who live in glass houses should not throw stones.

10. Alex likes to watch movies that have a lot of action.

11. Jennifer wore a scarf that matched her coat.

12. The student who studied the hardest did the best.

13. He bought all the tools that he needed for the project.

14. I bought the CD that Trevor recommended.

15. The girl who is standing in line is my cousin.

Using Pronouns That Ask Questions

Directions Choose the pronoun from the Word Bank that correctly
completes each sentence. Write the pronoun on the line.

EXAMPLE <u>Whom</u> did you call?

Word Bank
what
which
who
whom
whose

1. _________________________ is going with Brandon to the dance?

2. _________________________ shoes did Sarah buy?

3. _________________________ is the name of that book?

4. _________________________ backpack is this?

5. _________________________ is the capital of your state?

6. _________________________ CD did you borrow?

7. To _________________________ did you give the gift?

8. Riley asked _________________________ you are eating for lunch.

9. _________________________ is the new president?

10. _________________________ is the capital of Kentucky—Louisville or Frankfort?

11. _________________________ is your favorite flavor?

12. _________________________ color do you prefer—blue or yellow?

13. _________________________ is your favorite movie star?

14. _________________________ sweater is hanging in the closet?

15. _________________________ is the topic of this book?

Identifying Demonstrative Pronouns

Directions Underline the demonstrative pronoun in each sentence. Then decide whether the pronoun is singular or plural. Write *singular* or *plural* on the line.

EXAMPLE Does <u>this</u> belong to you? _______ singular _______

1. Picasso painted that in 1908. _________________________

2. Is that the train to Dallas? _________________________

3. Caleb found these in his locker. _________________________

4. This is the best river for canoeing. _________________________

5. Those are the girls who gave me a ride to work. _________________________

Directions Underline the pronoun that correctly completes each sentence.

EXAMPLE Is (<u>this</u>, those) shirt new?

6. Did you hear (this, that) noise?

7. I am making spaghetti for dinner. Do you like (those, that)?

8. Alex held up a book. "Is (this, that) yours?" he asked Daniel.

9. "(These, That) are my favorite shoes," said Amanda.

10. "(This, These) is my new puppy," said Julian.

11. Steve bought two bananas. "(These, That) make a good snack," he said.

12. (This, These) package just arrived.

13. (That, Those) is our new car.

14. "Did you see (those, these) deer?" asked John.

15. Did you see (that, this) shooting star?

Using Indefinite Pronouns

Directions Ten indefinite pronouns appear in the puzzle. The pronouns may be across, down, backward, or diagonal. Find them and list them on the lines. Then use each one in a sentence. The first one is done for you.

```
A  N  O  T  H  I  N  G  M  G  H  I
N  A  O  B  C  D  A  E  U  F  N  J
Y  Q  P  B  O  N  N  M  C  L  O  K
B  R  S  S  O  M  E  T  H  I  N  G
O  T  V  T  W  D  X  F  Y  Z  E  A
D  D  H  E  N  O  Y  R  E  V  E  B
Y  E  C  E  I  K  N  A  L  W  K  E
R  F  G  H  J  B  A  L  B  L  B  R
W  E  I  N  N  O  M  G  W  K  B  W
```

<table>
<tr><td colspan="2">Word Bank</td></tr>
<tr><td>another</td><td>nobody</td></tr>
<tr><td>anybody</td><td>none</td></tr>
<tr><td>everyone</td><td>nothing</td></tr>
<tr><td>few</td><td>something</td></tr>
<tr><td>many</td><td></td></tr>
<tr><td>much</td><td></td></tr>
</table>

1. <u>Anybody: Anybody can use the phone.</u>

2. _______________________________________

3. _______________________________________

4. _______________________________________

5. _______________________________________

6. _______________________________________

7. _______________________________________

8. _______________________________________

9. _______________________________________

10. ______________________________________

Recognizing Pronouns in Contractions

Directions Underline the contractions in each sentence. Then write each contraction as two words on the line.

EXAMPLE <u>You'll</u> have a lot of work with a new puppy. __________ You will __________

1. Who's your veterinarian? _______________________

2. Dr. Miller is good and he's right in town. _______________________

3. What's your dog's name? _______________________

4. I've had to hide all my shoes. _______________________

5. They're my pup's favorite toys. _______________________

6. We've put up gates in the kitchen. _______________________

7. That's where the puppy sleeps. _______________________

8. We're teaching our pup tricks. _______________________

9. He's learning to fetch a ball. _______________________

10. It's funny to watch him roll over. _______________________

11. I'd like to teach him to sit. _______________________

12. I'm reading a book about dog training. _______________________

13. I'll loan it to you after I finish reading it. _______________________

14. You'll learn some dog-grooming techniques. _______________________

15. We're glad we adopted a puppy. _______________________

Identifying Adjectives

Directions Find the adjectives in each sentence and underline them. Then draw an arrow from the adjective to the word it describes. *The, a,* and *an* are always adjectives. Do not underline them for this exercise.

EXAMPLE The bright red flowers cheered up the patient.

1. Cardinals like to live in thick woods.

2. Young children love to feed wild birds during the cold weather.

3. I like my pumpkin pie hot and sweet.

4. The cat's soft fur invited petting.

5. The cold water was refreshing.

6. Laura, smart and sweet-tempered, is a popular girl at school.

7. "Where is that large, heavy box that they delivered?" asked Gary.

8. After the swim in the lake, Dina felt cool and relaxed.

9. "Where did you buy this delicious cake?" Natasha asked.

10. A bushy, brown squirrel climbed up the tall oak tree.

11. Alex is funny, polite, and cheerful.

12. Julio is tired and grumpy.

13. Cammy adores her sweet puppy.

14. Because the weather was freezing, everyone came inside for hot cocoa.

15. The ice cream, tasty and cold, hit the spot after the long walk.

Identifying and Using Articles

Directions Underline the definite and indefinite articles in each sentence.

EXAMPLE <u>A</u> thesaurus and <u>an</u> almanac were on the library shelf.

1. An unusual silence came over the crowd.

2. The president and a senator will attend the ceremony.

3. Evita will bring a punch bowl for the party.

4. The forest fire destroyed a hundred acres of trees.

5. George put a radio, a compass, and an orange in the backpack.

Directions Decide whether *a, an,* or *the* correctly completes each sentence. Write the correct article on the line.

EXAMPLE Stacy did not know <u>the</u> best route.

6. Do you have __________ envelope that I can use?

7. Did you see __________ books I left here?

8. Look at __________ bluebird outside the window.

9. I would like to have __________ drink of water.

10. What happened to __________ house while we were away?

11. The recipe calls for __________ egg and some flour.

12. Sandy's trip to Japan was __________ exciting adventure.

13. Today my brother drove for __________ first time.

14. __________ hundred years ago, only a few people had telephones.

15. For the holiday, Justin's family had __________ elegant party.

Using Proper and Common Nouns as Adjectives

Directions Underline the proper adjective in each sentence. On the line, write the sentence and capitalize the proper adjective.

EXAMPLE Did you see my <u>french</u> book?   Did you see my French book?

1. He was eating in a chinese restaurant.

____

2. Later the class would study spanish culture.

____

3. Michael prefers swiss cheese on his ham sandwich.

____

4. Laura wrote a poem about her german ancestors.

____

5. We will take a european vacation after the holidays.

____

Directions Decide if the word in bold is a noun or an adjective. Write *noun* or *adjective* on the line.

EXAMPLE Jason bought a **class** ring.   adjective

6. The **basketball** court was covered in snow. _______________

7. George enjoyed playing **basketball.** _______________

8. We enjoy walking in the **park.** _______________

9. Let's rest on the **park** bench. _______________

10. The family enjoys a **salad** for lunch. _______________

11. Marge bought a new **salad** bowl. _______________

12. The **computer** room is crowded today. _______________

13. The students were waiting to use a **computer.** _______________

14. The temperature is below average this **winter.** _______________

15. School closed early due to the **winter** storm. _______________

Using Possessive Nouns and Pronouns as Adjectives

Directions Write each sentence on the line. Write the correct possessive form of each noun in parentheses.

EXAMPLE The (jet) crew was well trained. _______ The jet's crew was well trained. _______

1. The (students) play impressed the drama teacher.

   ____

2. There is (Mike) house.

   ____

3. (Luke) bag got lost at the airport.

   ____

4. The government should regulate the (companies) prices.

   ____

5. The (bus) passengers got off at the art museum.

   ____

6. The factory polluted the (lake) water.

   ____

7. Many people love the (choir) concerts.

   ____

8. David listened to his (mother) advice.

   ____

9. The (children) toys were scattered everywhere.

   ____

10. (Michael) bike has a flat tire.

    ____

Directions Decide whether the possessive pronoun *its* or the contraction *it's* correctly completes each sentence. Write the correct word on the line.

11. The bear is caring for _______ cub.

14. _______ too nice to stay inside today.

12. Damon wonders if _______ going to rain all summer.

15. Karen thinks _______ easy to run two miles.

13. My coat lost two of _______ buttons.

Using Numbers and Indefinite Pronouns as Adjectives

Directions The indefinite pronoun is underlined in each sentence. Replace each indefinite pronoun with a number used as an adjective. Write the new sentence on the line.

EXAMPLE <u>Many</u> people attended the meeting.   Forty people attended the meeting.

1. Eric had <u>some</u> reasons for not calling.

2. The TV station has a <u>few</u> camera operators.

3. Jeremy speaks <u>several</u> languages.

4. <u>Several</u> weather forecasters predicted the blizzard.

5. A <u>few</u> students wrote essays about folk art.

6. The company donated enough food to feed <u>many</u> people.

7. <u>Some</u> band members signed autographs after the concert.

8. A <u>few</u> people walked dogs in the park early in the morning.

9. <u>Several</u> models posed for the photographer.

10. Every summer, <u>many</u> families visit this amusement park.

Directions On the line, write the noun that each adjective in bold describes.

EXAMPLE Our neighbors have **two** dogs.   dogs

11. The recipe calls for **three** cups of flour.

12. The library has **thirty-three** autobiographies.

13. The Texas flag has **one** star.

14. Ian had saved **three hundred** dollars for the ski trip.

15. The band has **six** members.

Using Demonstrative Adjectives

Directions Find the demonstrative adjective in the Word Bank that completes each sentence. Write the demonstrative adjective on the line.

EXAMPLE I think <u>that</u> bird over there is a cardinal.

1. The stories in _____________ book are more exciting than the ones in these books.

2. Take _____________ flowers in my hand to your grandmother.

3. _____________ desk is bigger than the ones over there.

4. _____________ curtains need to be cleaned.

5. Look at _____________ sandwich!

Word Bank

that

these

this

those

Directions For each sentence, write the demonstrative adjective and the word it describes on the line. If a sentence does not have a demonstrative adjective, write *none*.

EXAMPLE Susan bought this vase in China. ________ this—vase ________

6. That hat is very warm. ________________________

7. Trevor finally found that camera. ________________________

8. He will check this shelf while you check those shelves. ________________________

9. Here are the notes from geography class. ________________________

10. Sandy is looking for a blouse to match this skirt. ________________________

11. Many customers trust that mechanic. ________________________

12. A lot of people stay at this resort. ________________________

13. The artist often used those colors. ________________________

14. That porch is shadier than this porch. ________________________

15. The author will write more about these characters. ________________________

Using Adjectives to Make Comparisons

Directions Write the form of each adjective in bold. Write *positive*, *comparative*, or *superlative* on the line.

EXAMPLES Bananas taste **better** than pears.   comparative
           Sam is the **tallest** boy in the room.   superlative

1. Why is Alex **angry** today? _______________

2. Isn't Tara the **sweetest** person? _______________

3. Rhode Island is **smaller** than Texas. _______________

4. The snowstorm today is **worse** than the one yesterday. _______________

5. Laura is my **best** friend. _______________

6. Prince is the **friendliest** of all the puppies. _______________

7. Carlos is **taller** than his brother Miguel. _______________

8. Monica is a **faster** sprinter than anyone else. _______________

9. The leaves are bright **red** this fall. _______________

10. Autumn is the **most beautiful** season. _______________

11. Please be **more careful**. _______________

12. Let's try to be **nicer** to each other. _______________

13. Angela's grades in English are very **good.** _______________

14. Van is a **friendly** person. _______________

15. That house is **less expensive** than mine. _______________

16. Is that bike too **large** for you? _______________

17. We purchased a **new** car last month. _______________

18. Science is Pamela's **best** subject. _______________

19. Of the three students, Donald is **tallest.** _______________

20. Andrea is **older** than Jennifer. _______________

Using Action Verbs

Directions Complete each sentence with an action verb. Write the action verb on the line. Use vivid, specific verbs.

EXAMPLE The basketball player <u>slams</u> the ball through the hoop.

1. The detective _____________ for clues in the alley.

2. The dancer _____________ gracefully across the stage.

3. A full moon _____________ over the city.

4. Donald _____________ his glasses in the library.

5. Snowflakes _____________ and _____________ on the mountainside.

6. A colorful kite _____________ over the trees.

7. The huge truck _____________ around the corner.

8. Jackie _____________ that painting.

9. On the beach, many people _____________ or _____________.

10. Lauren and Julie _____________ in the stylish store.

11. Joanna _____________ the ball to the catcher.

12. Natasha will _____________ her new book.

13. A row of flags _____________ on the city street.

14. A big fish _____________ out of the lake.

15. Chad and Keith quickly _____________ their lunch.

Directions Exchange papers with a partner. Look at the action verbs your partner used. Write a new sentence using each action verb from your partner's paper. Write your sentences on the back of this sheet.

Using Simple and Perfect Tenses

Directions On the short line, write each verb in the tense shown. Then use each verb in a sentence. Write the sentence on each long line.

EXAMPLE reach—future tense _________ will reach _________
The train will reach the station this afternoon. _________

1. dance—past tense

2. scream—past perfect tense

3. discover—future tense

4. plan—future perfect tense

5. frame—present perfect tense

6. cook—past perfect tense

7. drain—past tense

8. join—present perfect tense

9. measure—past perfect tense

10. decorate—present tense

Identifying Irregular Verbs

Directions Each sentence contains a verb error. Find the error. Then write the sentence with the correct verb form on the line.

EXAMPLE Juan has began to volunteer at the hospital.
<u>Juan has begun to volunteer at the hospital.</u>

1. Jim said he knowed the answer.

____

2. Kurt has went to the grocery store twice this week.

____

3. Dorothy has ate too much pizza tonight.

____

4. The dam bursted, and water flooded the valley.

____

5. Marcus seen a bear while he was camping.

____

Directions Fill in the blanks with the missing tenses. Write either the present, past, or past particle tense of each word on the line.

	Present	**Past**	**Past Participle**
6.			has bent
7.	eat		
8.		hid	
9.	is		
10.		flew	

Using Progressive Forms

Directions Complete each sentence. On the line, write a progressive verb phrase in the tense shown. Your verb must end in *-ing*.

EXAMPLE Eileen <u>has been searching</u> for an old edition of *Little Women*.
(present perfect progressive)

1. The traffic _________________ on the main highway. (present perfect progressive)

2. The girls _________________ a salad for dinner. (present progressive)

3. That tree _________________ for a hundred years. (future perfect progressive)

4. Kyle _________________ in the marathon. (past perfect progressive)

5. Students _________________ all day Saturday. (future progressive)

Directions Underline the progressive verb phrase in each sentence. Write its tense on the line.

EXAMPLE Carmen is running in a relay. _________ present progressive _________

6. Jack is washing his new car. _______________________

7. Last week George was fishing for bass in Lake Erie. _______________________

8. We will be leaving for our vacation in August. _______________________

9. Has everyone been doing their homework regularly? _______________________

10. The children had been thinking about the party. _______________________

11. Our family is flying to Daytona Beach in February. _______________________

12. Laura will have been living here for three years in June. _______________________

13. Lois and Dick were whispering in class. _______________________

14. By noon, the students will have been waiting for three hours. _______________________

15. The movie is beginning at seven o'clock. _______________________

Making Subjects and Verbs Agree

Directions Find the word in the Word Bank to complete each sentence.
Write your answer on each line.

EXAMPLE Lijing <u>seems</u> sad today.

1. The doctors _______________ to the emergency room.

2. My brother _______________ to be a doctor someday.

3. The outfielders _______________ baseballs very well.

4. Every morning, Dan _______________ to catch the bus.

5. Leslie _______________ excited about the changes.

6. Hay _______________ the floor of the barn.

7. Kelly _______________ a cold every winter.

8. I _______________ you get the job you want.

9. The people _______________ to like this musician.

10. Blankets _______________ all of the good furniture.

Word Bank
catch
catches
cover
covers
hope
hopes
hurry
hurries
seem
seems

Directions Underline the verb form that correctly completes each
sentence.

EXAMPLE Both Mike and Jenny (<u>like</u>, likes) oranges.

11. All of us (are, is) going to the movies.

12. Everyone (are, is) invited to the party.

13. One of the students (were, was) on time.

14. Alex (go, goes) to the mall on weekends.

15. Jack (enjoy, enjoys) watching football.

16. Several of the girls (paint, paints) for fun.

17. One of the players (are, is) sick today.

18. Everyone (go, goes) to the dentist.

19. All of the varieties of bread (taste, tastes) fresh today.

20. The students (were, was) prepared for their test.

Using the Verb *Do*

Directions Read each sentence. Write the verb or verb phrase on the line.
Decide whether the verb *do* is used as a main verb or a helping verb. Write
main verb or *helping verb* on the line.

EXAMPLE Darren does not often watch TV.   _______ does watch—helping verb _______

1. Most people do not enjoy loud music. _______________

2. Does anyone have a piece of gum? _______________

3. Allen's brother does his laundry in the dormitory. _______________

4. Casey did a sculpture for the art show. _______________

5. Luke does the family's dishes each day. _______________

6. Did you write that date on your calendar? _______________

7. The comedy group had done a skit about UFOs. _______________

8. The store will do a lot of business over
   the weekend. _______________

9. Do you agree with the newspaper editorial? _______________

10. We will have done our biology homework
    by lunchtime. _______________

11. The patient does not remember the accident. _______________

12. Each week, the critic does a review of a new
    movie. _______________

13. Did her voice remind you of Jennifer? _______________

14. I do not like to talk about politics. _______________

15. The club members do a different service project
    each year. _______________

Using Conditional Verbs

Directions Underline the verb or verb phrase that correctly completes each sentence.

EXAMPLE James (<u>could have</u>, could of) been hurt in the fire.

1. The team (should of, should have) finished practice by now.

2. Melody said, "(Can, May) we have a picnic in the park?"

3. A calculator (might, might have) been helpful for that activity.

4. The coach told them to run five miles if they (could, can).

5. Dina (should have, should) practiced before the race.

6. Dennis thought he (could, can) see the Big Dipper.

7. Morris (would have, would) liked that movie.

8. Someone (must of, must have) turned off the lights.

9. Anne (would have, would) volunteered for the job.

10. Justin said, "(Can, May) you pick me up after school?"

Directions Write a sentence on the line using each verb or verb phrase.

EXAMPLE could be deciding
     <u>The principal could be deciding whether to cancel the field trip.</u>

11. might have returned

____

12. should be leaving

____

13. will have answered

____

14. shall pretend

____

15. must have believed

____

Identifying Active and Passive Verbs

Directions The verb or verb phrase in each sentence is in bold. Decide whether it is active or passive. Underline your answer.

EXAMPLES That picture **was painted** by my mother. (Active, <u>Passive</u>)
My mother **painted** that picture. (<u>Active</u>, Passive)

1. Susan **packed** her suitcase for the trip. (Active, Passive)

2. The music **was played** beautifully by the school orchestra. (Active, Passive)

3. Andy's keys **were found** in the gym. (Active, Passive)

4. The treasure **was found** in a cave. (Active, Passive)

5. The students **played** the game three times. (Active, Passive)

6. The garden **was watered** this morning. (Active, Passive)

7. A bird **flew** into the barn. (Active, Passive)

8. The lions **snarled** at each other. (Active, Passive)

9. The meal **was prepared** by Alison's mother. (Active, Passive)

10. The melody **was played** by the clarinets. (Active, Passive)

11. Those flowers **were eaten** by a rabbit. (Active, Passive)

12. My cat **had been chased** by a dog. (Active, Passive)

13. I **met** my new neighbors today. (Active, Passive)

14. Beth **painted** a portrait of the queen. (Active, Passive)

15. Mary **hit** a homerun. (Active, Passive)

16. Jim **kicked** the extra point. (Active, Passive)

17. The tree **was struck** by lightning. (Active, Passive)

18. Larry **was chased** by a bear. (Active, Passive)

19. Mr. Tibbetts **drove** the bus. (Active, Passive)

20. The statue **was made** of bronze. (Active, Passive)

Identifying State-of-Being Verbs

Directions Underline the state-of-being verb or verb phrase in each sentence.

EXAMPLE Alex and Tom <u>are</u> good friends.

1. Alex and his friend Tom are in Washington.

2. The apples in Washington are very fine.

3. They taste better than most apples.

4. Washington apples look especially inviting.

5. The apple tasted terrific to Alex.

6. He had become an apple expert.

7. Tom seemed happy with the trip.

8. He appeared especially joyful to Alex.

9. "Have you become a fan of Washington apples also?" asked Alex.

10. "I have grown fonder of them recently," laughed Tom.

11. Alex and Tom felt tired from their trip.

12. "We should look our best tomorrow," said Alex.

13. Our meeting with the governor is at noon.

14. "We could easily be there at noon," said Tom.

15. Alex and Tom remained at the apple orchard for a while.

16. The apples tasted too good to leave.

17. "They get better every year," said Alex.

18. "They look better, too," said Tom.

19. "I feel very full," said Alex.

20. Both boys are definitely apple lovers.

Exploring State-of-Being Verb Tense

Directions Write the correct form of the verb *be* on each line. Refer to the chart below.

	I	**he/she/it**	**you/we/they**
Present	am	is	are
Past	was	was	were
Future	will be	will be	will be
Present Perfect	have been	has been	have been
Past Perfect	had been	had been	had been
Future Perfect	will have been	will have been	will have been

EXAMPLE Susan and Frank <u>are</u> at the mall.

1. In the fall, Susan will _________________________ at a horse show.

2. Susan _________________________ excited about entering her horse, Kat.

3. Kat _________________________ a blue-ribbon winner last year.

4. Kat's talent _________________________ high stepping.

5. Kat has _________________________ in many horse shows.

6. On the day of the show, Susan's parents will _________________________ there.

7. Her friend Frank will _________________________ in the first row.

8. Kat will have _________________________ in 12 shows after this one.

9. All of Susan's friends have _________________________ supportive.

10. Susan has _________________________ nervous before each show.

11. Sometimes she _________________________ not nervous at all.

12. "Where have you _________________________?" asked Frank.

13. "I have _________________________ to shows all over the United States," said Susan.

14. When Kat pranced into the show ring, Susan _________________________ calm.

15. If Kat wins a blue ribbon, Susan and her horse will have _________________________ winners again.

Identifying Verbs as Action or State of Being

Directions Decide whether the verb in bold expresses action or a state of being. Underline the correct answer for each sentence.

EXAMPLE She **smelled** the flowers.   <u>action</u> being
The flowers **smell** good.   action <u>being</u>

1. Jason **remained** after the others had left.
action   being

2. Jim and Randy **remained** friends for years.
action   being

3. Gail **felt** excited.
action   being

4. The children **felt** the first drops of rain.
action   being

5. The Browns **grow** pumpkins every year.
action   being

6. Yuri **grew** three inches this year.
action   being

7. Kim **looks** tired today.
action   being

8. Did you really **look** for your shoes?
action   being

9. Carol's perfume **smelled** nice.
action   being

10. Can you **smell** her perfume?
action   being

11. The coffee **smelled** inviting.
action   being

12. Marcy just **got** a new car.
action   being

13. The weather suddenly **got** colder.
action   being

14. Nathan **keeps** his comb in his pocket.
action   being

15. This cheese **keeps** fresh for a month.
action   being

16. Miguel just **became** the owner of a turtle.
action   being

17. I **tasted** everything at the party.
action   being

18. Everything **tasted** good to me.
action   being

19. Fred **appears** tired today.
action   being

20. Donna suddenly **appeared** in the room.
action   being

Identifying Adverbs

Directions Underline the adverbs in these sentences.

EXAMPLES I will answer your e-mail <u>soon</u>.
The turtle crawled <u>slowly</u> down the road.

1. Earl whispered softly.

2. The big horse won the race easily.

3. Please talk quietly in the hall.

4. Paul's sister often reads stories to him.

5. You told that story well.

6. Did you put your gloves here?

7. I will do the dishes promptly.

8. Finally the storm ended.

9. The wind blew loudly all night.

10. The child ran happily down the path.

11. I thought the dancers moved gracefully.

12. They tiptoed lightly around the house.

13. Suddenly the lightning flashed.

14. We waited breathlessly for the answer.

15. Danny did his homework carefully.

16. She spoke crossly to her friends.

17. The speaker talked quickly.

18. Mr. Smith chuckled gleefully.

19. Willis will go next.

20. Meg works quickly.

Finding Adverbs of Degree

Directions Underline the adverb of degree in each sentence. Circle the
word the adverb of degree describes. If that word is an adjective, write
adjective on the line. If the word is an adverb, write *adverb*.

EXAMPLE The monument was <u>rather</u> (large.)   adjective

1. Your eyes look so blue today.

2. Maurice seemed extremely angry.

3. Karen only occasionally remembers to call.

4. Caleb very rarely goes to the movies.

5. She was completely sure they were finished.

6. Norm just barely fit in the small car.

7. Laura was especially tired after the game.

8. Only two rooms are available at the hotel.

9. Luke nearly always forgets his umbrella.

10. Very little help is available for this problem.

Directions Add an adverb of degree to each sentence. Write the new
sentence on the line.

EXAMPLE The lemonade is refreshing.   The lemonade is quite refreshing.

11. A quiet woman sat down beside me.

12. Donald rides that bus frequently.

13. The weather became cool.

14. The divers came to the surface rapidly.

15. Laura's painting seemed old-fashioned.

Identifying Adverbs of Negation

Directions Read the following paragraph. Circle each adverb of negation. The first one is done for you.

Jeremy had thought he could never enjoy painting. However, his mother didn't give him a choice. He could not talk her out of it. Jeremy had never tried anything creative. When he started painting, though, he didn't want to stop. His art teacher said she had never taught such a talented student. She entered one of Jeremy's paintings in a citywide art contest, although he did not believe his work was good enough. He did not believe her when she told him he had won first prize. Jeremy was happy. He wouldn't have succeeded if his mother and his teacher had not encouraged him.

Directions Circle the adverb of negation in each sentence.

EXAMPLE Cheryl never said anything about her appointment.

1. Alex couldn't have imagined such a hot day.

2. There was never any ice cream in the Murphys' freezer.

3. The garden has never looked more beautiful.

4. The company won't release any information about the accident.

5. The hikers didn't have any way to keep warm in the woods.

6. The sun never came out all day.

7. Julio wouldn't sing for his family.

8. Jack can't remember the words to the song.

9. We couldn't get tickets to the concert.

10. I am not having dessert tonight.

Using Adverbs to Compare

Directions Circle the adverb in each sentence. Then write its form—
positive, *comparative*, or *superlative*.

EXAMPLE ___comparative___   Gordon finished his dinner (more quickly) than his brothers.

_______________________ **1.** Martin played the harmonica brilliantly.

_______________________ **2.** Stacy and her partner ran the three-legged race least clumsily.

_______________________ **3.** My neighbor treats her children generously.

_______________________ **4.** Amber completed the test speedily.

_______________________ **5.** The kayakers are paddling more energetically now.

_______________________ **6.** The latest computer model performed best.

_______________________ **7.** Anita could draw better after she took an art class.

_______________________ **8.** Did these tools exist earlier?

_______________________ **9.** Mike swam farther from shore.

_______________________ **10.** People move more slowly in hot weather.

Directions Add *-ly* to each word. Write the new word on the line. Then
write a sentence using the word as an adverb.

EXAMPLE poor   <u>poorly</u>   <u>Jason skates poorly when he forgets to warm up.</u>

11. loud   _______________________   _______________________________

12. bright   _______________________   _______________________________

13. glad   _______________________   _______________________________

14. kind   _______________________   _______________________________

15. sad   _______________________   _______________________________

Recognizing Adverbs

Directions Decide whether the word in bold in each sentence is an adjective or an adverb. Write *adjective* or *adverb* on the line.

EXAMPLES We take a **weekly** magazine. _______ adjective _______
The child giggled **happily**. _______ adverb _______

1. Andy looked up **eagerly**.

____

2. Alice took the **early** bus to the city.

____

3. The wind blew **wildly** all night.

____

4. Our family has **partly** finished eating the pudding.

____

5. The daily newspaper was **late**.

____

6. I **hastily** sent an e-mail.

____

7. Speak **calmly** to the frightened child.

____

8. Certain plants contain **deadly** poisons.

____

9. Danny found a **wriggly** earthworm in the garden.

____

10. People pay certain taxes **annually**.

____

11. Treat the pony **gently**.

____

12. The wrecked car was a **ghastly** sight.

____

13. Nancy bought some **crinkly** paper to wrap the gift.

____

14. The speaker gave his speech too **rapidly**.

____

15. The music that the band played was **lively**.

____

16. I think the sweater is too **costly**.

____

17. That was a **silly** remark!

____

18. Mr. Bacon chuckled **cheerfully**.

____

19. The story I heard was most **unlikely**.

____

20. Mrs. Peterson is a very **friendly** neighbor.

____

Identifying Prepositions

Directions Choose a preposition that correctly completes each sentence. Write the preposition on the line. You may use words from the box to the right.

EXAMPLE The children <u>on</u> the swings are laughing.

Prepositions	

about
above
across
after
around
at
before
behind
beneath
beside
down
during
for
from
in
into
near
of
off
on
out
over
past
through
to
under
until
with

1. The man _______________________ the porch is my father.

2. Cheesecake _______________________ strawberries is a tasty treat.

3. My friend _______________________ Los Angeles just bought a puppy.

4. The picture _______________________ the wall brightens up the room.

5. A picture _______________________ Juanita is in the frame.

6. The star _______________________ the play got a standing ovation.

7. The young man _______________________ Susan is her cousin.

8. The peaches _______________________ the tree are ready to pick.

9. The players _______________________ the football field are doing their best.

10. The house _______________________ the lake is for sale.

11. The movie _______________________ the theater starts at 8:30.

12. The house _______________________ mine is painted purple.

13. My friend, Nancy, lived _______________________ Colorado.

14. Trish ran _______________________ the bridge.

15. Sarah will stay _______________________ we finish.

Recognizing the Object of the Preposition

Directions Underline the prepositional phrase or phrases in each sentence. Then draw an arrow from each preposition to its object.

EXAMPLE The guests are on the porch.

1. My father and I ate dinner with our friends at a restaurant.

2. Cynthia found the dictionary for Rick.

3. She rode the roller coaster at the amusement park.

4. The Gibsons live in a small town in the southern part of Ohio.

5. The dog chased the rabbit down the path and into the field.

6. Jane received a birthday card from Luke.

7. The skater fell down on the ice.

8. Did this button fall off your coat?

9. In 10 minutes, the team scored eight points.

10. Carol is selling tickets to children at the carnival.

11. We crossed over the highway and walked into the woods.

12. Look behind the door for your umbrella.

13. The rocket shoots into the sky.

14. The bridge was built over a large river.

15. Bob wrote an essay about folk music.

16. Robin found a book from the library under the sofa.

17. We had a snack in the meeting room during the break.

18. Steve lives near a large lake.

19. Boots, our cat, sleeps on the window sill in the living room.

20. Gloria gave a present to Bob for his birthday.

Recognizing Adjective Phrases

Directions Underline the adjective phrases in these sentences. Then draw an arrow from each adjective phrase to the noun or pronoun it describes.

EXAMPLE The house <u>on the corner</u> is for sale.

1. Wimbledon is a tennis tournament in England.

2. Most of the world's best players participate.

3. All of the matches in the tournament are exciting.

4. The play by Pete Sampras has been wonderful to watch.

5. Many of his serves have made the audience gasp.

6. Wimbledon tennis courts with their grass surfaces are different.

7. Men with powerful serves usually win the tournament.

8. The best woman player in the world won the match.

9. She is now a publisher of a tennis magazine.

10. The most famous tennis tournament in America is the U.S. Open.

11. The largest mammal in the world is the blue whale.

12. My dog is the winner of the contest.

13. The tree in my yard is very big.

14. Brent showed me a bird in a tree.

15. He is the king of the world.

Adding Adverb Phrases

Directions Each verb or verb phrase in these sentences is in bold. Add an
adverb phrase to each sentence, and write the new sentence on the line.
Underline the adverb phrase.

EXAMPLE We **left.**   _______ We **left** <u>in a hurry</u>. _______

1. The lady **bought** a new bike.

____

2. Everyone **joined** the exercise class.

____

3. The snow **was falling** lightly.

____

4. The puppy **barked** excitedly.

____

5. The store **opens** early.

____

6. Sally **will be** there.

____

7. Bully, the St. Bernard puppy, **barked** loudly.

____

8. Bake us a chocolate cake.

____

9. Carla **wrote** a short story.

____

10. The teacher **asked** the class a question.

____

11. The old man **talked** to me.

____

12. My best friend **eats** peanut butter.

____

13. The bird **chirped.**

____

14. The boy and his bicycle **went** fast.

____

15. The computer **worked** well.

____

Using Prepositional Phrases Correctly

Directions Find the word in the Word Bank to complete each sentence.
Write your answer on each line. Be sure that the verb you choose agrees
with the subject of the sentence.

EXAMPLE The boy in the corner <u>speaks</u> very softly.

1. The theater in the mall _________________________ closed.

2. The boys on the track _________________________ very fast.

3. The girl at the table _________________________ very quickly.

4. Many stores in the mall _________________________ closed.

5. One of my cousins _________________________ very fast.

6. The cars on the lot _________________________ for sale.

7. The rabbits in the cage _________________________ quite often.

8. The frog in the pond _________________________ very far.

9. The salad in the cafeteria _________________________ great.

10. The men at the school _________________________ many languages.

11. One girl in my class _________________________ rugby.

12. The boys in my class _________________________ soccer.

13. The man at the store _________________________ me shoes.

14. The women at the store _________________________ me clothes.

15. The owner of the store _________________________ me "hello."

Word Bank
are
has
have
hop
hops
is
play
plays
run
runs
sell
sells
speak
speaks
tells

Identifying Prepositions and Adverbs

Directions Read each sentence. Decide whether the word in bold is a preposition or an adverb. Write *preposition* or *adverb* on the line.

EXAMPLES Put the cat **out!**   adverb
            Look **out** the window.   preposition

1. The dog's toy was **underneath** the sofa. _______________

2. Look **underneath.** _______________

3. Throw the ball **up** higher. _______________

4. My house is **up** the street. _______________

5. From the top of the Empire State Building, the cars **below** were tiny. _______________

6. The subway train runs **below** the ground. _______________

7. The skater fell **down** on the ice. _______________

8. The rain rushed **down** the gutters rapidly. _______________

9. Look **outside** and see the lightning. _______________

10. **Outside** the window we saw the lightning. _______________

11. I'd like some honey **in** my tea, please. _______________

12. Bring the dog **in** right now! _______________

13. The dog is **in** his house. _______________

14. Let's throw the ball **around** before the game. _______________

15. The players threw the ball **around** the bases. _______________

Using Coordinating Conjunctions

Directions Read the pairs of sentences below. Use a coordinating conjunction to join the sentences. Write the sentence on the line. You may need to change the verb form.

EXAMPLE Toby had soup for lunch. Toby also had salad.
<u>Toby had soup and salad for lunch.</u>

1. Plain water is sugar-free. It is also caffeine-free.

____

2. My older brother, Casey, plays soccer. My little brother, Jimmy, plays soccer.

____

3. My favorite baseball player is Derek Jeter. My other favorite player is Roger Clements.

____

4. Toni Morrison wrote *Beloved*. She wrote *Tar Baby*.

____

5. I have a poodle named Velvet. I have a poodle named Buffy.

____

6. Velvet is black. Buffy is white.

____

7. My garden has roses. It has ivy. It has herbs.

____

8. My friend Mary enjoys sewing. She also enjoys reading.

____

9. For the picnic, we bought potato salad. We bought hot dogs.

____

10. Betty likes hot dogs. She doesn't like hamburgers.

____

11. Tim rides a bike. Tim can't drive a car.

____

12. I like the color blue. I like the color red. I like the color green.

____

13. My mother likes watching mysteries. My mother doesn't like watching sports.

____

14. My house is white. My house has blue shutters.

____

15. Seth is my son. Ryan is my son.

____

Using Correlative Conjunctions

Directions Read the following sentences. Write the correlative conjunction in each sentence on the line.

EXAMPLE Both the time and the place of the next meeting will be posted.
         <u>Both . . . and</u>

1. Sasha has exams Tuesday in both algebra and biology.

____

2. You may use either a clock with a second hand or a stopwatch.

____

3. Neither the bank nor the post office is open on Thanksgiving.

____

4. Mr. Yan is both my advisor and my teacher.

____

5. Dad said to turn off either the CD player or the TV set.

____

6. Alex not only played in the game but he also made the winning goal.

____

7. Both my brother and my sister like to sing.

____

8. You may either take this bus or wait for a later one.

____

9. Whether you catch the first bus or the second, you should arrive on time.

____

10. Not only is Sarah the class president, but she is also on the soccer team.

____

Directions Read each pair of sentences. Underline the correct sentence.

EXAMPLE   **A**   <u>Both the national anthem and "America, the Beautiful" were sung.</u>
         B   Both the national anthem and "America, the Beautiful" was sung.

11.   **A** Neither the gym nor the cafeteria is open now.
     B Neither the gym nor the cafeteria are open now.

12.   **A** Not only Luke but also his younger sisters take violin lessons.
     B Not only Luke but also his younger sisters takes violin lessons.

13.   **A** Neither the Senate nor the House of Representatives meet today.
     B Neither the Senate nor the House of Representatives meets today.

14.   **A** Both Stephen and Maria tutor younger students.
     B Both Stephen and Maria tutors younger students.

15.   **A** Either Liza or Scott live in that house.
     B Either Liza or Scott lives in that house.

Recognizing Subordinating Conjunctions

Directions Underline the subordinating conjunction in each sentence.

EXAMPLE Ms. Rodriguez will ride in the parade <u>since</u> she is on the city council.

1. Lisa bought paints so that she could create a sign for the garage sale.

2. Rob said he would go wherever we want to go.

3. No planes will be able to take off tonight if the blizzard strikes.

4. Will you call me when you arrive?

5. President George Washington retired to Mount Vernon when he left office.

6. Even though it is the largest state in land area, Alaska has very few people.

7. Because it was raining, the baseball game was canceled.

8. The relay runner grabbed the baton as it was passed to her.

9. The artist did not want anyone to see her painting before it was completed.

10. Although she was just a student, Maya Ying Lin designed the Vietnam Veterans Memorial.

Directions Use a subordinating conjunction to connect each pair of sentences. Write each sentence on the line. Then underline the dependent clause in each new sentence.

EXAMPLE Our team cannot win. We score another touchdown.
Our team cannot win <u>unless we score another touchdown</u>.

11. Sara baby-sat for three hours. She can earn enough money to buy a CD.

____

12. The movie began at 7:00 PM We didn't arrive at the theater until 7:10 PM.

____

13. I met José at the library. We could study together.

____

14. The President gave a speech. He took the oath of office.

____

15. The groundhog saw its shadow. It came out of its hole on February 2.

____

Using Interjections

Directions Write each sentence using correct punctuation and capitalization.

EXAMPLES
No you can't go with them today	No, you can't go with them today.
Whew that was close	Whew! That was close!
Hey stop that	Hey! Stop that.

1. Oh no I forgot to turn off the oven.

2. Oh that waterfall is breathtaking.

3. Hello is anyone there?

4. Alas they are tearing that beautiful old house down.

5. My goodness I am sleepy.

6. Well maybe I can finish this project by then.

7. Wow what a great gift it's just what I wanted.

8. Yum that stew smells wonderful.

9. Hurry we are going to be late again.

10. Nonsense you don't really think I would believe that.

11. Hey where do you think you're going?

12. Oh woe is me I am so sad today.

13. So what who cares if you're mad?

14. Slow down you are driving too fast.

15. Brr I'm freezing.

Recognizing Sentences

Directions Underline the groups of words that are sentences. Circle the groups of words that are sentence fragments.

EXAMPLES <u>Rabbits ate the vegetables.</u>
Need to build a fence.

1. Monkeys in trees.

2. Living on a farm in New Jersey.

3. Blueberries are good for you.

4. Have you ever tasted a loganberry?

5. Tastes sweet and tart.

6. Went to the airport.

7. He invited his cousin to visit him.

8. A kangaroo has a pouch to carry babies.

9. To protect their young.

10. Ancient Egyptians believed cats were sacred.

11. Make their own clothing.

12. A bear lives in a den.

13. A pack of wolves hunting together.

14. The Sears Tower is a tall building.

15. An elephant's tusks are made of ivory.

Finding Subjects in Sentences

Directions Underline the complete subject in each sentence.

EXAMPLE <u>All of these programs</u> are on during the day.

1. Soap operas first became popular on the radio.

2. People sat around their radios and listened to the stories.

3. Many of the sponsors were soap companies.

4. Daytime dramas were therefore nicknamed soap operas.

5. One famous soap opera was called *Our Gal Sunday.*

6. Your grandmother probably knows about this program.

7. Another popular program in the 1940s was *The Romance of Helen Trent.*

8. My grandfather's favorite program was *One Man's Family.*

9. *One Man's Family* was an evening soap opera.

10. It was on the radio for many years.

11. That program moved to TV in the late 1950s.

12. Today people still like soap operas.

13. You have probably heard of *General Hospital.*

14. Soap opera stars are very popular.

15. People watch the shows and talk about their favorite characters.

Adding the Predicate of a Sentence

Directions Each group of words below is a sentence fragment. Complete each sentence by adding a predicate.

EXAMPLE Clara Barton
<u>Clara Barton founded the Red Cross.</u>

1. The car with the flat tire _______________________.

2. The entire class _______________________.

3. The mayor of our town _______________________.

4. The test on Monday _______________________.

5. My favorite TV program _______________________.

6. My best friend and I _______________________.

7. The students in this class _______________________.

8. Our school basketball team _______________________.

9. Thanksgiving dinner _______________________.

10. The small town in Idaho _______________________.

11. The flower in the vase _______________________.

12. The new student _______________________.

13. My new computer _______________________.

14. The red car _______________________.

15. The monkeys at the zoo _______________________.

Identifying the Purposes of Sentences

Directions Decide the purpose of each sentence. Write *statement,* *command,* *question,* or *exclamation* on the line. Then, rewrite each sentence using correct punctuation.

EXAMPLES Where is the bus?   _______question_______

Please shut the door.   _______command_______

1. Does Joel know where we are   ______________________________

____

2. Mr. Nicholson has gone to the dentist   ______________________

____

3. We are leaving now   ______________________________

____

4. Please give Jesse the book   ______________________________

____

5. Does Ben know you are here   ______________________________

____

6. Hey be very careful with the vase   ______________________________

____

7. We are having stew for supper   ______________________________

____

8. Did Diane win the math prize   ______________________________

____

9. The tickets are for sale   ______________________________

____

10. This game is so exciting   ______________________________

____

Identifying Simple and Compound Sentences

Directions Read the following sentences. Write *S* on the line if the
sentence is a simple sentence. Write *C* if it is compound sentence.

EXAMPLES ___C___ The boys washed the car, and they worked in the yard.
___S___ Pat walked to the museum.

__________ **1.** Mr. Remsburg and the class visited a laboratory.

__________ **2.** There were powerboats and sailboats at the dock.

__________ **3.** My cousins and my uncle are camping at the lake.

__________ **4.** Louis had a map, but he still got lost.

__________ **5.** Look under the porch, and then look in the garage.

__________ **6.** I think Kevin is funny, and I know he is intelligent.

__________ **7.** Those dogs bark too much, and they also chase my cat.

__________ **8.** Cara and Leslie went to buy groceries and clothes.

__________ **9.** Where have the boys put the mustard and the relish?

__________ **10.** Chuck made a list, but he forgot to bring it.

__________ **11.** Our family saw the Washington Monument and visited
the White House.

__________ **12.** David went shopping, but he didn't buy anything.

__________ **13.** I need to buy a notebook, and I also need to get
a package of pencils.

__________ **14.** Mark ran around the track and practiced jumping.

__________ **15.** We made a cake and bought some pizza.

Using Intransitive Verbs

Directions Write the simple subject and the verb or verb phrase for each sentence.

	Simple Subject	**Verb or Verb Phrase**
EXAMPLE The train to Baltimore has departed already.	train	has departed

	Simple Subject	**Verb or Verb Phrase**
1. The president's speech will be televised.		
2. Some birds chirped noisily.		
3. My friend will study with me.		
4. Who can work at the bake sale on Saturday?		
5. We will walk in the parade.		
6. Plates and glasses suddenly crashed onto the floor.		
7. Did the team practice yesterday?		
8. George Washington lived in Virginia.		
9. The doctors worked in the hospital.		
10. Our music teacher has performed on Broadway.		
11. Paul, David, and Mike went to Steve's house.		
12. Steve served nachos to his friends.		
13. The boys watched TV.		
14. Steve's mom lives in Idaho.		
15. The boys listened carefully.		

Diagramming Sentences with Intransitive Verbs

Directions Write a sentence using each intransitive verb or verb phrase.

1. went ____

2. dream ____

3. sat around the house ____

4. ran quickly ____

5. read ____

Directions Underline the intransitive verb or verbs in each sentence.

6. The boys went to the store.

7. James and Larry ran down the street.

8. The woman in the red sweater walks home.

9. George sings and dances.

10. Alex eats slowly, so we waited for him.

Directions Each of these diagrams matches a sentence from above. Select
the correct sentence for each diagram. Complete the diagrams.

11. 

12. 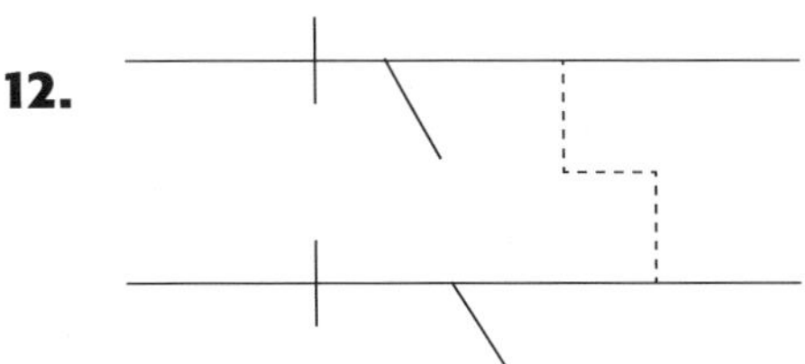

13. 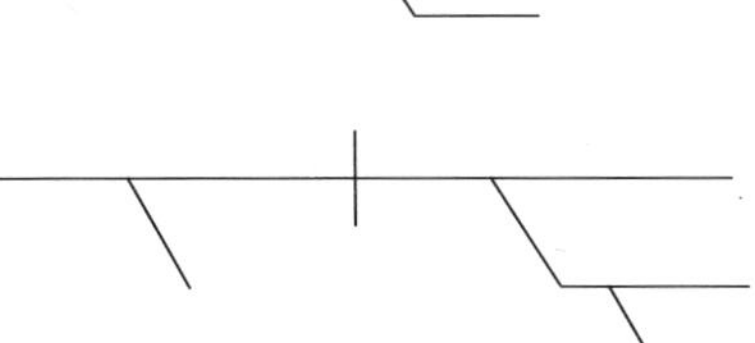

14. 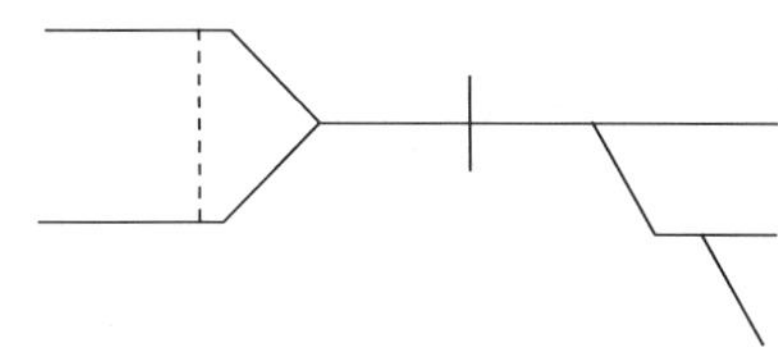

15. 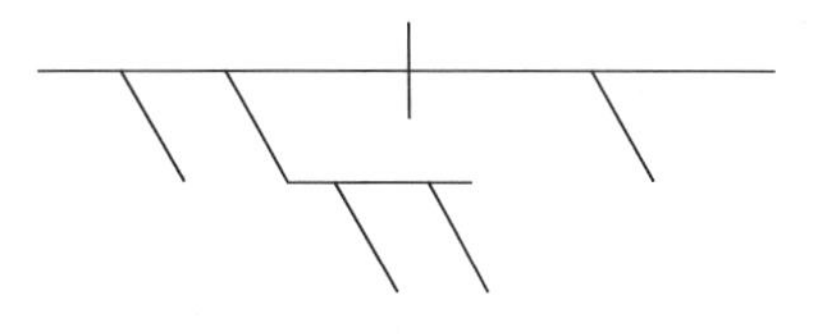

Using Direct Objects

Directions Underline the verb or verb phrase in each sentence. Then,
write the direct object on the line.

EXAMPLE Kevin <u>plays</u> the drums in a band. _________ drums _________

1. Alison baked cookies for her friends. _____________________

2. Paul frequently reads books about space exploration. _____________________

3. The musicians played the piece perfectly. _____________________

4. That factory produces computers. _____________________

5. Grace made a skirt and wore it to the party. _____________________

6. The farmers will harvest wheat in the summer. _____________________

7. The students collected donations. _____________________

8. Please push them on the swings. _____________________

9. We met Janice and her sister at the mall. _____________________

10. Did you bring your lunch? _____________________

Directions Choose the pronoun in parentheses that correctly completes
each sentence. Write the pronoun on the line.

EXAMPLE Brian invited (him, he) to dinner. _________ him _________

11. Linda followed (me, I) to the bookstore. _____________________

12. Tell (she, her) about the telephone call. _____________________

13. Where should (we, us) put our coats? _____________________

14. The photograph showed (she, her) at the beach. _____________________

15. Mr. Choy directed (they, them) to the principal's office. _____________________

Diagramming Sentences with Direct Objects

Directions Write a sentence using each direct object.

1. Katie, Maggie _______________________________________

2. dog ____

3. polar bear _______________________________________

4. school ____

5. enchiladas _______________________________________

Directions Underline the direct object in each sentence.

6. My mother made steaks for dinner.

7. Did you find your wallet?

8. Eat your mashed potatoes.

9. Tammy won a new car and drove it to school.

10. Jack studied history, and Maria studied science.

Directions Each of these diagrams matches a sentence from above. Select the correct sentence for each diagram. Complete the diagrams.

11. 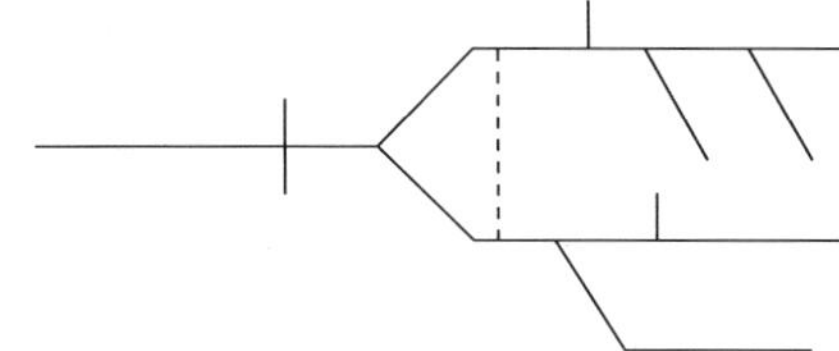

12. 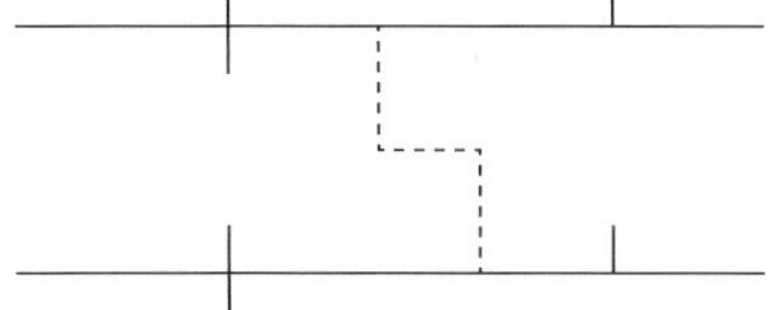

13.

14. 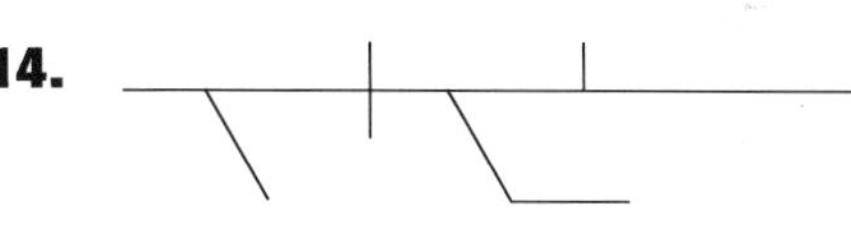

15. 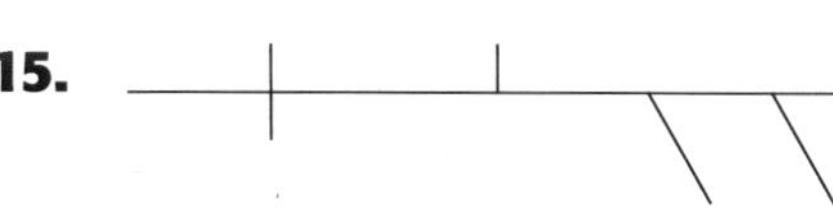

Using Indirect Objects

Directions Underline the direct object in each sentence. Then, write the indirect object or objects on the line.

EXAMPLE Samantha poured him a <u>glass</u> of iced tea.   <u>   him   </u>

1. Send your mother some flowers.   _______________________

2. Did that movie give you the chills?   _______________________

3. Jessica showed Kurt and me her art project.   _______________________

4. Ryan read his friends a story.   _______________________

5. Her grandmother wrote her a poem for her birthday.   _______________________

6. The weather report gave us information.   _______________________

7. The pitcher threw the batter a curveball.   _______________________

8. Sasha wrote her cousin a long letter.   _______________________

9. The librarian brought them several books.   _______________________

10. Todd tossed Jason the ball.   _______________________

Directions Add an indirect object to each sentence.

EXAMPLE Beth told ___us___ a good joke.

11. John sold _________________ his old computer.

12. That school offered _________________ a scholarship.

13. The store issued _________________ a refund.

14. Please lend _________________ your support.

15. Mr. Giles built _________________ a swing set.

Diagramming Sentences with Indirect Objects

Directions Write a sentence using each indirect object.

1. Sarah ____

2. them ____

3. me ____

4. Carlos and Rodrigo ____

5. the dog ____

Directions Underline the indirect object in each sentence.

6. Rebecca gave her a pretty scarf.

7. Can you get me a drink?

8. Gloria gave Betty a book about photography.

9. Jack and Sam gave Molly a picture.

10. I gave my son a toy.

Directions Each diagram matches a sentence from above. Select the correct sentence for each diagram. Complete the diagrams.

11.

12.

13.

14.

15.

Using Object Complements

Directions Underline the direct object in each sentence. Write the object complement or complements on the line.

EXAMPLE The scientists found the <u>question</u> puzzling. _______ puzzling _______

1. The dye stained his hands orange.

   ____

2. Call the game a tie.

   ____

3. The teacher called David dependable.

   ____

4. Cynthia calls *Great Expectations* her favorite book.

   ____

5. Ms. Clute made Garrett her assistant.

   ____

6. Don't make the chili too spicy.

   ____

7. Road construction made drivers nervous.

   ____

8. Many people consider their computers important.

   ____

9. Liza found the job difficult yet fun.

   ____

10. They named the baby Kelly.

    ____

Directions Complete each sentence by writing an object complement on the line.

EXAMPLE Melissa called the color _______ mustard _______.

11. The people elected John Thomas
    _______________________.

12. Critics consider the play
    _______________________.

13. Everyone declared the chili recipe
    _______________________.

14. The committee pronounced the conference
    _______________________.

15. The police considered the suspect
    _______________________.

Diagramming Sentences with Object Complements

Directions Write a sentence using each object complement.

1. red ____

2. excellent ____

3. president ____

4. quick ____

5. crunchy, messy ____

Directions Underline the object complement in each sentence.

6. Tommy colored the picture bright purple.

7. Did you find the movie funny?

8. Elect Richard Romero the leader.

9. Boys and girls find the new movie exciting.

10. The board elected Tom president and Jeremy vice president.

Directions Each diagram matches a sentence from above. Select the correct sentence for each diagram. Complete the diagrams.

11.

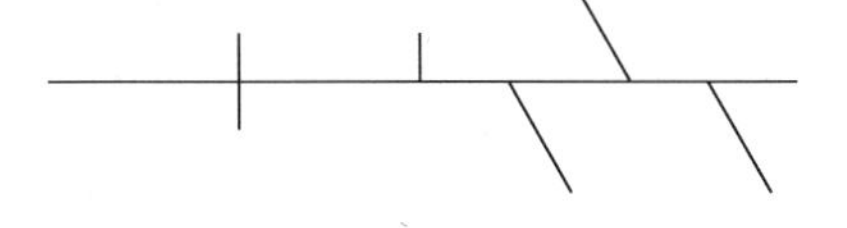

12.

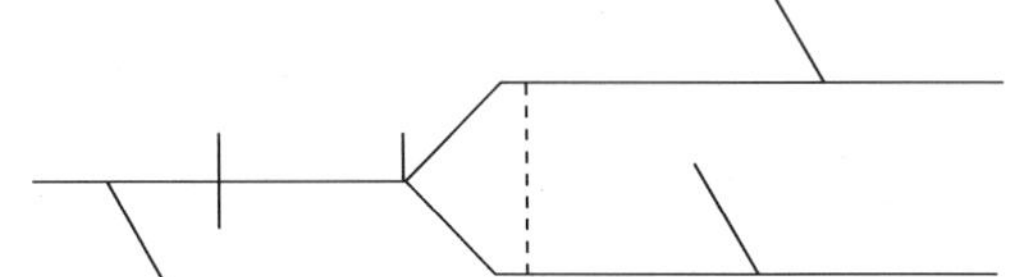

13.

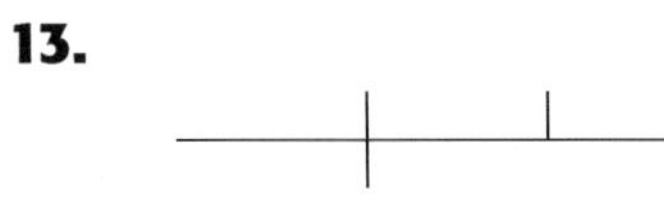

14.

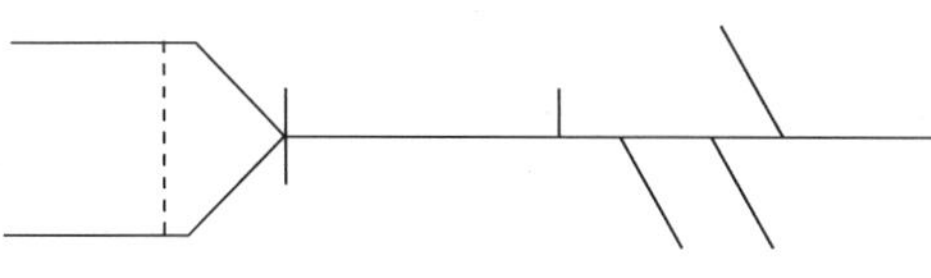

15.

Using Predicate Nouns

Directions Underline the linking verb or verb phrase in each sentence.
Then write the predicate noun on the line.

EXAMPLE *American Gothic* <u>is</u> a masterpiece.   masterpiece

1. The next performer will be Lisa.   _______________

2. The dictionary remains an important book.   _______________

3. The *Star Wars* films have been a huge success.   _______________

4. The Statue of Liberty remains a powerful symbol.   _______________

5. *The Hobbit* is Alex's favorite novel.   _______________

6. *Cats* is a well-known musical.   _______________

7. Dana will become a lawyer.   _______________

8. Aunt Charlotte has always been an enthusiastic
   quilter.   _______________

9. Professional athletes are role models for
   young people.   _______________

10. Margaret Thatcher was a prime minister in
    Great Britain.   _______________

Directions Complete each sentence by writing a predicate noun that
renames the subject. Include adjectives if needed.

EXAMPLE Quinn became a good _____writer_____.

11. My sister is a
    _________________________.

12. One fun activity in winter is
    _________________________.

13. A famous monument in Washington, D.C., is
    _________________________.

14. A hero to many young people is
    _________________________.

15. One of the greatest inventions is
    _________________________.

Diagramming Sentences with Predicate Nouns

Directions Write a sentence using each predicate noun.

1. coach ____

2. piano ____

3. Francis ____

4. giraffe ____

5. leader ____

Directions Underline the predicate noun in each sentence.

6. Ryan is a wonderful artist.

7. Is that your notebook?

8. Be a good class leader.

9. Justin is an author and an illustrator.

10. Sales is my current job, but my dream is modeling.

Directions Each of these diagrams matches a sentence from above. Select the correct sentence for each diagram. Complete the diagrams.

11. 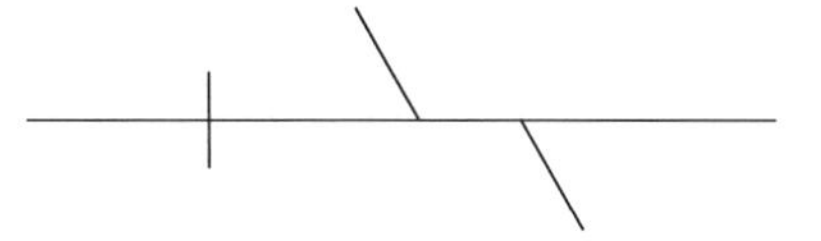

12. 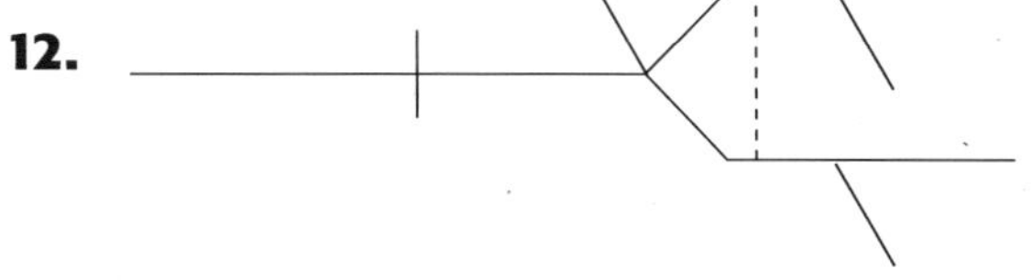

13.

14. 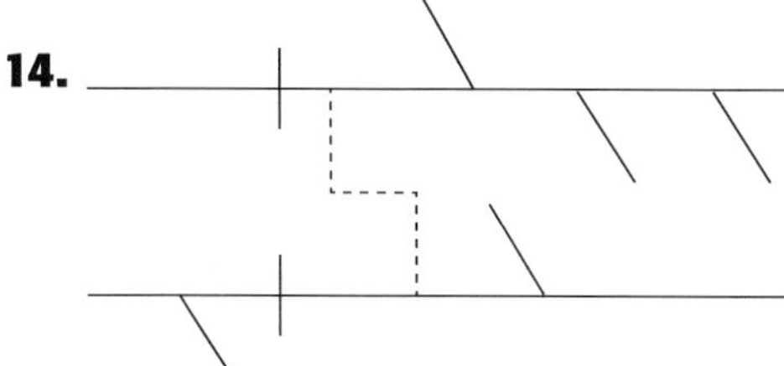

15. 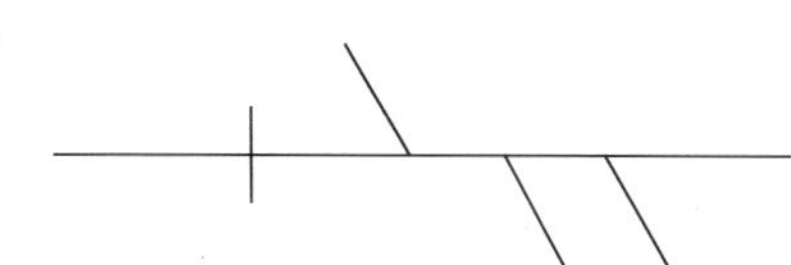

Using Predicate Adjectives

Directions Underline the linking verb in each sentence. Then write the predicate adjective or adjectives on the line.

EXAMPLE That motor <u>seems</u> very powerful.　　　　_______ powerful _______

1. The movie was fun and exciting. _________________

2. The mountain roads became dangerous in a storm. _________________

3. A delicate coral reef was visible beneath the waves. _________________

4. That stamp may be extremely valuable. _________________

5. Was the travel route convenient for you? _________________

6. Jeannie looked shaken after her fall. _________________

7. Several of us became tired after the game. _________________

8. Kevin's vivid dream seemed real. _________________

9. The drawings of the insects were precise. _________________

10. Our celebration was quiet but enjoyable. _________________

11. The comedy troupe was fun and lively. _________________

12. The air felt damp and chilly inside the cave. _________________

13. That chair looks ragged yet comfortable. _________________

14. Maria feels energetic after her exercise class. _________________

15. The children's feet were bare at the beach. _________________

Diagramming Sentences with Predicate Adjectives

Directions Write a sentence using each predicate adjective.

1. dark, stormy ____

2. slimy ____

3. sad ____

4. nearly impossible ____

5. quite exciting ____

Directions Underline the predicate adjective in each sentence.

6. The soup tasted wonderful.

7. The chocolate was very messy.

8. Was the new book quite interesting?

9. Be smart.

10. The food was good, but the service was poor.

Directions Each of these diagrams matches a sentence from above. Select the correct sentence for each diagram. Complete the diagrams.

11. 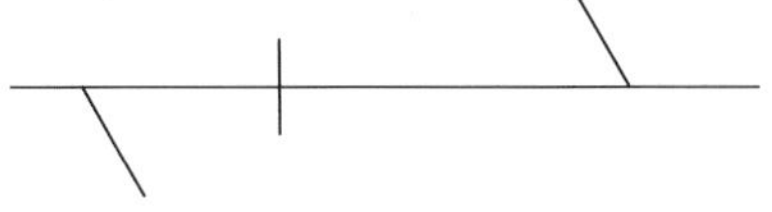

12. 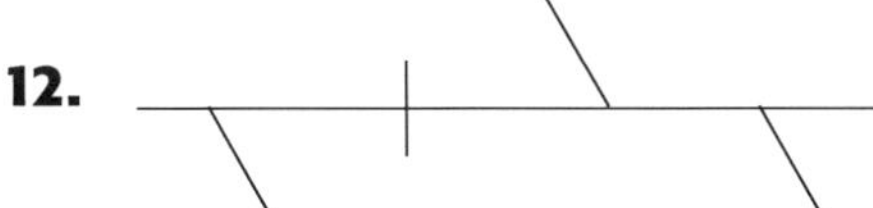

13. 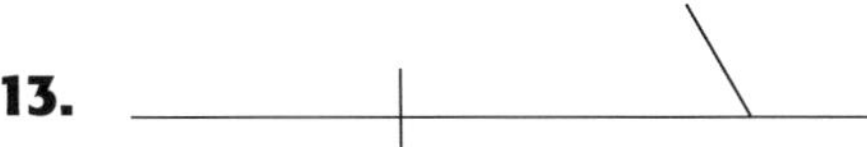

14. 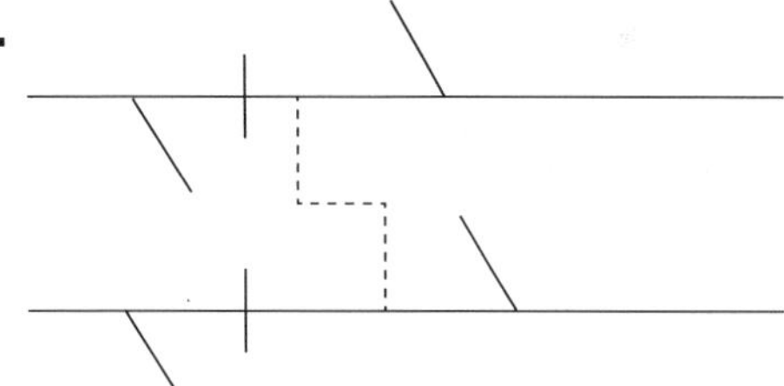

15. 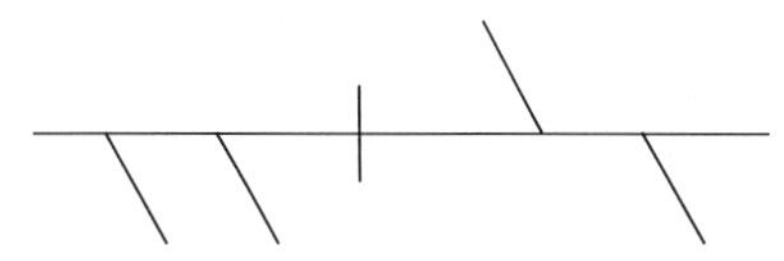

Using Phrases and Clauses

Directions Decide whether each group of words in bold is a prepositional phrase, dependent clause, or an independent clause. Write the correct label above the words.

dependent clause
EXAMPLES **After the game was over,** the team ordered pizza.

prepositional phrase
We drove quickly **through the tunnel.**

1. **After Jeannie read the book,** she wrote a report.

2. **Because she was locked in her stall,** my horse was feeling restless.

3. Sharon found her lost bracelet **under the bed.**

4. **Before we left the game,** we said good-bye to our friends.

5. **Mr. Johnson took the class to a museum.**

6. **Sarah left the party early** because she felt ill.

7. **From the top of the hill,** I could see all of the countryside.

8. **My friend Bindu visited New Orleans** on her vacation.

9. Michael missed school **because of the flu.**

10. **If the movie ends soon,** can we go for ice cream?

11. **What will the coach do** if his team does not win the game?

12. I saw a deer **on the edge of the clearing.**

13. The child **who won first place** is a wonderful musician.

14. After they set up their tents, **the campers built a fire.**

15. My sister decided not to drive **because the road was under construction.**

Identifying Adverb Clauses

Directions Underline the adverb clause in each sentence.

EXAMPLE Mike went home <u>when the rain started</u>.

1. Howard plans to go to work after he graduates from high school.

2. Our new house has more rooms than the old house had.

3. After I learned to play tennis, it became my favorite sport.

4. Jack worked as hard as he could.

5. Gail could hardly wait until the holidays arrived.

6. Yuli always knew where she put her slippers.

7. Until a computer is available, you can work with me.

8. Max joined the band because he likes music.

9. Rusty answers his e-mail whenever he can.

10. Is Marge younger than Richard is?

11. Get some sleep if you are tired.

12. The field was wet after it rained.

13. The skater did many jumps because he wanted to win.

14. Charlotte swims faster than Alice does.

15. When you learn the rules, the game will be easy.

Using Noun Clauses

Directions Underline the noun clause in each sentence. On the line, write whether the noun clause is a subject, direct object, indirect object, object of the preposition, predicate noun, or object complement.

EXAMPLES   The new computer is just <u>what I needed</u>.   <u>predicate noun</u>
          Please tell me <u>what you want</u>.   <u>direct object</u>

1. The blue sweater is exactly what I wanted. _______________________

2. Name the puppy whatever you like. _______________________

3. That computer is what I want. _______________________

4. Show whoever you want my photographs. _______________________

5. Does anyone know what those people are doing? _______________________

6. Whoever finishes first wins the race. _______________________

7. We gave whoever wanted one a ride on the go-cart. _______________________

8. Whoever is hungry should come and eat. _______________________

9. The teacher said that my poster had won the contest. _______________________

10. Everyone asked who would be at the party. _______________________

11. Whatever you decide is fine. _______________________

12. Did Alison hear what you said? _______________________

13. You should let me know what you want. _______________________

14. What you said is very important. _______________________

15. The teachers brought pencils for whoever needed one. _______________________

Identifying Appositives and Nouns of Direct Address

Directions Find the word in the Word Bank to complete each sentence. Write your answer on the line. Be sure that the word you choose makes sense.

Word Bank

book
David
doctor
Miss Landis
myself
sister
son
song
Stacy
teacher

1. Julia, my _________________________, is a doctor.

2. _________________________, you are needed in the ER now!

3. Who sings "It's a Wonderful World," my favorite _________________________?

4. _________________________, be nice to your sister.

5. A girl in my class, _________________________ is very smart.

6. My brother, _________________________, likes to race motorcycles.

7. I, _________________________, am afraid of motorcycles.

8. Miss Landis, my _________________________, is very nice.

9. _________________________, can I help you?

10. *To Kill a Mockingbird*, the _________________________, is wonderfully written.

Directions Read each sentence from above. Decide whether the word you chose is an appositive or a noun of direct address. Write your answers on the lines below.

11. _________________________   16. _________________________

12. _________________________   17. _________________________

13. _________________________   18. _________________________

14. _________________________   19. _________________________

15. _________________________   20. _________________________

Identifying Adjective Clauses

Directions Underline the adjective clause in each sentence. Then write the word that the adjective clause describes on the line.

EXAMPLE Martin is the player who <u>scored the most baskets</u>.   player

1. The watch that my mother gave me is beautiful. _______________

2. Are you the man whom I met at the library? _______________

3. Carol asked Danny, who was her friend, to the party. _______________

4. The gift that John gave his mother was for her birthday. _______________

5. The question that she asked did not make sense. _______________

6. My aunt bought a computer that has a built-in modem. _______________

7. April, who plays soccer, loves the game. _______________

8. Patience is the one who takes care of their pets. _______________

9. The man whose wife works at the library is our baseball coach. _______________

10. Bill bought the CD that Jenna suggested. _______________

11. We stayed in a hotel that had a pool. _______________

12. The contest that Kathy won had a prize of $100. _______________

13. Danny organized the notes that he had taken. _______________

14. The boy who was allergic to peanuts refused to eat the candy. _______________

15. The geese that live here are beautiful. _______________

Identifying Complex Sentences

Directions On each line, write a complex sentence using the words in bold.

EXAMPLE **read** <u>I love to read mystery novels before going to sleep.</u>

1. **racing** ____

2. **bugs on the ground** _______________________________________

3. **school bus** ____

4. **tacos** ____

5. **report card** ____

6. **birthday party** ____

7. **the planet Mars** ____

8. **breakfast** ____

9. **favorite car** ____

10. **the best song** ____

11. **Saturday morning cartoons** _______________________________________

12. **scary movies** ____

13. **the soccer ball** ____

14. **my best friend** ____

15. **the pounding rain** ____

Identifying Compound-Complex Sentences

Directions Decide whether each sentence is simple, compound, complex or compound-complex. Write the answer on the line.

EXAMPLES Alice lives in Florida. _______ simple _______
Alice lives in Florida, but she always vacations in Maine. _______ compound _______
My friend, who lives in Florida, always vacations in Maine. _______ complex _______

1. Tonya wrote me a letter when I was gone, but the postal service sent it back.

____

2. The sky was dark, but it didn't rain.

____

3. All of the neighbors attended the party.

____

4. Baltimore, which is in Maryland, is fun to visit, but we don't get there often.

____

5. After the party was over, everyone helped to clean up.

____

6. Because of the party, we met new people.

____

7. People have been talking about a party.

____

8. If we have a party, will you come?

____

9. Did you know anyone who was there?

____

10. I knew many people, and had a good time.

____

11. The sunset, which was bright orange, was pretty, but we weren't ready to go in.

____

12. One of the neighbors provided entertainment.

____

13. Dave, a firefighter, does magic tricks.

____

14. He normally charges a fee, but he performed that night for free.

____

15. Brad will sleep if you let him, but it's time to get up.

____

16. He brought a rabbit that comes out of a hat.

____

17. Some of the neighbors were part of the act.

____

18. People loved when Dave disappeared.

____

19. Since the children cheered, he did more tricks.

____

20. Tammy likes steak if it's cooked well, but she prefers chicken.

____

Identifying Infinitives and Infinitive Phrases

Directions Read each sentence. Decide whether the words in bold are an infinitive or a prepositional phrase. Write the answer on the line.

EXAMPLES Carrie likes **to jog**. _______ infinitive _______

She went **to the park**. _______ prepositional phrase _______

1. Susan has been **to many shows**. _______________________

2. Susan wants **to join** the team. _______________________

3. She likes **to jump** her horse over fences. _______________________

4. The challenge is **to ride** smoothly. _______________________

5. You have **to practice** every day. _______________________

Directions Underline the infinitive phrase in each sentence.

EXAMPLE John hoped <u>to win a gold medal in the Olympics</u>.

6. Melissa loves to eat scrambled eggs with ketchup.

7. My grandmother wants everyone in her family to be happy.

8. Suki wants to see the polar bears at the zoo.

9. Kurt chooses to collect old toy cars.

10. To run for office, you must be in touch with the issues.

11. Jared doesn't like to dust his house.

12. Lilly wants to learn how to cook low-fat meals.

13. I like to go skiing in Colorado.

14. Candice likes to sleep late on Saturdays.

15. Karen wants to read.

Recognizing Gerunds and Gerund Phrases

Directions Underline the gerund phrase in each sentence. Decide whether the gerund phrase is used as a subject, direct object, object of the preposition, or predicate noun. Write the answer on the line.

EXAMPLE The family enjoys <u>camping at national parks</u>. ______ direct object ______

1. Kate wrote a report on exploring the oceans. ________________________

2. Chasing tornadoes is a dangerous job. ________________________

3. Jefferson helped by writing the Declaration of Independence. ________________________

4. Rita often imagined becoming an opera singer. ________________________

5. The counselor talked about applying to colleges. ________________________

6. Shoveling snow is hard work. ________________________

7. The puppy enjoyed tearing up newspaper. ________________________

8. Traveling across the United States was something Ed wanted to do. ________________________

9. Mark's favorite exercise is bike riding. ________________________

10. Marleen won a prize for painting a picture. ________________________

11. Seeing the mountains inspired me to write a poem. ________________________

12. Her job includes reporting on high school sports. ________________________

13. By volunteering at the center, you help your community. ________________________

14. Caring for pets is a big responsibility. ________________________

15. After planning our trip, we made flight reservations. ________________________

Identifying Participles and Participle Phrases

Directions Underline the participle or participle phrase in each sentence.
Then write the noun or pronoun it describes on the line.

EXAMPLE On the porch we found a kitten <u>licking its paws</u>. _______ kitten _______

1. The waving flags gave the city a festive air. ___________________

2. The class found the film entertaining. ___________________

3. We saw a fisherman standing on the rocks. ___________________

4. The girls found a puppy crying beside the road. ___________________

5. The idea described by Jason is an original one. ___________________

6. Walking quickly around the block, Carol was
   soon out of breath. ___________________

7. The frozen yogurt tasted delicious. ___________________

8. A raging hurricane struck the small island. ___________________

9. Sandy found the missing skirt in her closet. ___________________

10. The salad brought by Luisa contained walnuts. ___________________

Directions Make each verb below a participle. Then, use it in a sentence to
describe a noun. Write each sentence on the line.

EXAMPLE cheer   <u>Cheering crowds greeted the President.</u>

11. frighten ___________________

12. concentrate ___________________

13. mail ___________________

14. cook ___________________

15. catch ___________________